Gino Leineweber

HELLO DARKNESS

POEMS
2010 – 2014

Verlag Expeditionen

Publisher: Verlag Expeditionen GmbH
© Gino Leineweber 2017
Hello Darkness – Poems 2010-2014

Cover photo: Gino Leineweber
Cover Design: Birgitta Sjöblom
Text Editor: Barry Stevenson

ISBN 978-3-943863-58-1

For Dalia

Table of Contents

Hello Darkness

Romance

Table of Contents

Literature

HELLO DARKNESS

CHANGING ENERGY

As if lightning
Struck from the head to the toes
Running through your body
Making you wonder
If there is anything else left
Other than power

Nevertheless, you will never know
Whether the door to your heart has opened
Or your heart is totally gone
Even if you pass planet after planet
You are still wondering about the energy
But soon that is going to change again

BIRD

I am a bird
Without feathers
        A singer
        Without a voice
I do not fly
I do not sing
        But longing
        For a lifetime

I am a tree
Without branches
        A flower
        Without a bloom
I do not grow
I do not blossom
        But longing
        For a lifetime

If I were
A bird, a singer
A tree or a flower
        I would not
        Have wasted
        My potentials
                On a lifetime
                As a man

NEW MYTHOLOGY

Behind religions
the immortality of
All philosophies fades
Dwindling ideas:
Old mythologies
Loss images –
For every being
                    Their foundation Abstracted

Look deeper:
Infinity
The worlds run
Blank and void
New metaphor:
Ant!
Tulip in Tulips' Field
                    Every being Impermanent:

Galactic energy
Form and dynamics
Life and love
Acceptance of the movement.
Meditation
On the basic form
With all power
                    In the spiritual: Redemption

THOUGHTS

What you thought
In the first place
Was like the spell
Of a divine princess

That leads you to run around
Like an ancient bellman
Who has woken up
The entire town

Telling the world about
Your happiness
Shouting the solution
To all the suffering:

Love has survived!
But it turns out it was a trick
Of the black princess
In the mirror of disguise

To get laughs on idle nights

TRYING

I tried and tried
To love with my soul

I tried and tried
To love with my heart

I tried and tried
to notice my feelings

Nevertheless, still
I love with my eyes

SETTLED

A convenient life for most
Who never play the new
And also do not know
The many that have got lost

What will they call ideas
If they don't even know the end
And how the world is built
If the start has already gone

Everything around appears so far away
Every futile move is done
Why not deploy old rules
To birth, new life for everyone

INFIDELITY

October sun
Wall-height windows
The sea near by

It is not warm
He feels not cold but fear
She is wet

He strokes the desired body
With his tongue
A hand touches her breast

Tickles with fingers
The hard tips.
Moans of desire

She is ready
Widens herself
Opens to fraud

Scraps of guilt
Swirling his sensations
It was not right

NO WAY OUT

in every beginning
an ending is implied

cannot get one
without an other

cannot get
joy, excitement, happiness
without
sadness, frustration, suffering

have got life
gotten a beginning

DOVES

Formation flight
Two after each another
In circles
Then two after two
Flailing with the wind
Up in the air
Sailing down
Speedily but mellow
With serious faces
And utterly quiet

LOVE WAS NOT ENOUGH

Your face of a thousand faces
Your smile from a thousand eyes
And a thousand kisses from your lips

We were touchy-feely beings
We could not be apart
And filled our hearts with love

But love was not enough
Was it you? Was it me?
Who took away the energy?

MY SOUL

I left my soul behind
Now I have to wait
Or should I go back?

What if she's expecting me?
To come back?
Maybe she does

But why should I do so?
Imagine, I go back and
Meet her halfway in between

No, I won't go back
I won't wait either
I am not her slave

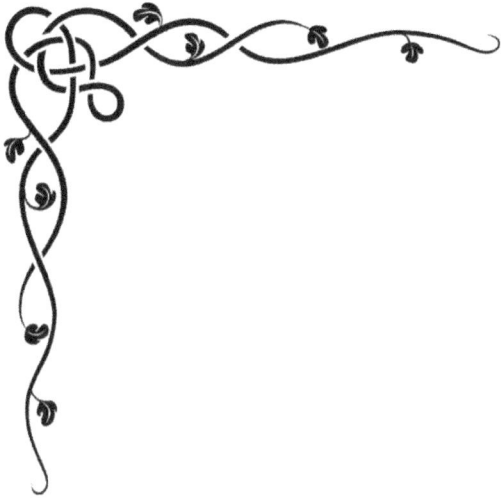

ROMANCE

ENDEARMENT

Cloud Mountains on the horizon
Enflamed by a tired sun,
Attendants heading home
Taverns at the shoreline
Turning on their lights
Waitresses ready to serve.
Later lovers passing by,
Whispers in the moonlight –
Kisses of endearment

PRETTY FACE

He first set eyes on her at the border
Heading for the Land of Wisdom
And became acquainted while walking and riding
And it wasn't only him that, from time to time,
Was, amid the group, glancing at her pretty face.
The first touch of her soft hand by accident
Made them laugh, caused the serene mood
Like a sunny island in both their interests
In literature, history, tasty food and talks
And still let him peek at her pretty face.
On the returning path to their homes
Caring fate brought them nearer, and her whisper:
Shall we sit together? caused him quivers almost
Of anticipation, so close, so longed for, so warm – but
On the plane he didn't dare to take her in his arms.
Farewell time under the mosaic ceiling
At the next airport led to the first embrace.
After a last hurrah with talks and coffee
It turned out, this pretty face
Belonged to his missing part.
The little arrow of the deity of love
Sailed thousands and thousands of miles
And over water from north to south
Her touches and her warmth and the smile
On her pretty face started to heal the cut.
But the gods, are still jealous of happiness
Were disturbing the atmosphere
With power that casts itself in different directions
So, to beware of drowning, he swims night after night
Looking for her pretty face on the other side

SPELL

Under her spell
Her mesmerizing voice
Softened and withdrew
From his male fantasies
Faded behind his closed eyes
With her whisper
He grew calm
Taking deep breaths
Enjoying slow
Gentle caresses
Having her intimately close
Smelling her musky odor
Feeling the moist of her lips
He drives away into the magic
Of a new experience
To lie in her arms
Was a divine pleasure
It made him shiver with ease
And incapable of escape
Her hands were gentle but firm
Her voice continued whispering
Soft and aware that he could not
Relinquish control
Or move or beckon to relax
Without her explicit order
Heaviness in his limbs as she cast
Over him the spell of immobility
He was eager for kisses
And waited to take off
To the peaks of heavenly pleasure

LITTLE RHODIAN PALETTE

Reflecting sunshine
On the green leaves
Of a banana tree
Shy walls hiding
Behind curls of
Lilac bougainvillea
Yellow-white insisting
For attention
A pretty frangipani
The magic of a smile
On your pretty face
Under a blue summer hat
The rosy Rhodian pebbles
Dreaming of you
By the Aegean sea

SHE TOLD ME

I asked for a phone
She told me

I asked for a post office
She told me

I asked for no more
She told me

From her eyes
She told me

Again these Eyes

After four years
Without a thought to find
What put him once
So amazingly
Under the spell

In bear-hunt time
This year
With all the
Colored leaves around
May be just a tiny wish…

Yet he is under a charm again
Again these eyes
Again his sight
That again he
Cannot take away

She neither
Although not the very same
But for these eyes
And now he
has a name

HAND

He knows he would
Have to inhale again
Breathing

Just not so quick
So quick

Breathlessly feeling
Feeling

Her hand
So soft, so gentle
So gentle

He exhales
Sighing, whining
At ease

He is breathing
And breathing
And faster

In the rhythm
Of her hand
Her hand

COUPLE

They are always
Hiding their names

Nevertheless
I want to know

A hint said he
Mine starts

With a G

Okay
Next said she

Mine with a D

Then smiled at me
Then at each other
Then kissing

kissing

kissing

SCENT

The dawn is

        Falling down

Into the room

        The smell of her skin

                Mingled with

        Night-flowers' scents

He is touching

        Almost instinctively

                Her delicate buds

                Sharpening his senses

        In growing

Lusty flavors

IGNITION

Light a fire
Of affection

Invite passion
For patience

Declare fortune
In missing

Put a string
Around her heart

SIGNIFICANT

the twilight is over...

speculation in

anticipation

whispers awaiting

answers

of course

waiting for

modification

the inevitable

LITERATURE

ERNEST HEMINGWAY

Like any writer he found words
Constructed sentences
And he put them on paper
On pages, in books
But he was one of the few
That dived deeper and deeper
Into the ocean of understanding
Finding the immortal words.
Coming back to the surface
The discrepancy was intolerable,
His true inner person couldn't survive
In the world of reconciliation –
Here he had to hide his emptiness
Pretending in daylight
That the nightmares of the cruelty of death
Were the strength of his life
This involved a lot of pretense,
Playacting and talking himself up
And these character traits
He possessed in abundance
As a young man he had already given his soul
To the deities of literature
Who rewarded him over and over
In finding the words he was looking for
Indeed, his tragic end would suggest
There was a price to pay.
The nature and style of his life
as a sacrifice for the writing

HORTON BAY

Horton, the man from the North
Looked around and intended
A better life with his family –
He had to sail to the south,

Yet, Lake Michigan is ocean-like water.
To avoid another shipwreck
When the wind blew for three days,
He left the boat and went on land

A second Three Days' Blow
Was seen as a sign from God
To stay on the ground at the bay
Even for years alone with the family

Then the lumberjacks came
Cutting trees, erecting mills
Founding the town
Naming it after him: Horton

When the trees were gone
People left and took away
What makes a mill a mill
And a town a town,

Five houses left on the main road
In a big grove of elm trees
Smith's, Stroud's, Dillworth's,
Horton', and Van Hoosen's

Plus the general store and post office,
The blacksmith shop was painted red
And faced the school
The road was very sandy

A migratory youngster wrote it down
The nature, the area, the town
Had his name carved
On the firmament of understanding

Later, beyond the horizon,
He lost his soul and missed
What makes a heart a heart
And a man a man

UP IN MICHIGAN

The three men are back from hunting
Now cheering, drinking
She is sitting on a kitchen chair
Waiting for him
The one she fell in love with

He approaches and kisses her
Strokes her breasts, says:
"Come on out for a walk"

Down on the point at the bay
She says no to him

But without avail
Heavy his body upon hers

Shortly after
He fell asleep

When she freed herself
From the burden
She takes care
Covers his body
With her coat
Tears in her eyes

Even the veil of innocence
Is torn apart
Her love does not stop
She tries to wake him
Wants to talk
Then going away
A cold mist
Comes up from the bay

INDIAN CAMP

There was a time when settlers
Invaded the homestead
Of the Aanishinaabek in Michigami
Intending to destroy
Their culture and religion
The lives of families and bands
Taking with betrayal after betrayal
Their harmony and breath
Exploiting the natives as workers
Bark peelers, berry pickers
Boxed up in Indian Camps
Intoxicated them with booze to compensate
For the lost horizon of hope
Scorning them for their fall
Into second-rate people
Erecting a nation on the remains.

After one of the Fourth of July festivities
A boy was travelling home
With the parents of friends
All along the way, their driver had to stop
To pull aside Indians lying on the road:
That's nine of them he says
Just between here and the edge of the town
And his wife replies: Them Indians

THE OLD MAN AND THE SEA

Blue is in the sky and in the water
Yellow tinted the village
The soil looks burned
An old man and a fish
But to no avail

It seems the angels themselves
Have operated the printing press
As the author gave his soul
For one last time
To an unforgettable book

Two-Hearted River

Day by day
Two branches floating
In the shadow of trees
Arriving at the mouth
Of the Lake Superior.

Here was a man
After trout,
A wounded mind
After a war,
Black Grasshoppers
After a fire.

Day by day
Two branches floating
In the shadow of trees.
The lyric name
Freeing the mind.

The man said:
"Go on hopper"

www.ingramcontent.com/pod-product-compliance
Lightning Source LLC
Chambersburg PA
CBHW020439030426
42337CB00014B/1329